Bygone London

Kevin McCormack

Ian Allan
PUBLISHING

Introduction

This colour album is a follow-up to *Streets of London*, first published in 2001, which depicted London some 40-50 years ago through the medium of buses, trolleybuses and trams. However, *Bygone London* is slightly different in not focussing entirely on these types of road vehicle but also on other forms of transport. Indeed, in a few cases the concept of movement is confined to pedestrians!

As well as being England's capital, London is, of course, one of the great cities of the world. Situated some 50 miles upriver from the Thames Estuary, London has spread beyond the original City (the 'Square Mile') to absorb immediately surrounding villages and those parts of the Home Counties administered by the London Boroughs. These are now regarded as London's suburbs and include some surprisingly rural areas.

There is an elected Mayor of London, whose responsibilities include the capital's public-transport system and who has decided to remove London's famous Routemaster buses from normal service after 50 years. There is also a Lord Mayor of London, a successor to Dick Whittington, whose appointment each year is celebrated by the Lord Mayor's Show, when he travels in his golden carriage in a spectacular procession. The Lord Mayor heads the City of London Corporation, the local authority responsible for the 'Square Mile' containing Britain's financial centre, which it actively promotes.

Front cover: **All lined up at Trafalgar Square and raring to go: two Austin taxis prepare to race RTL1214 to the top of the Whitehall straight. The splendid architecture visible in this August 1958 view consists of South Africa House, opened by King George V in 1933, the spire of St Martin-in-the-Fields church and, on the extreme left, the National Gallery.** *Ian Stewart*

Back cover: **Carter's Seeds had an imposing building near the railway line at Raynes Park and was still making deliveries to the station by horse-drawn cart when this picture was taken in 1959.** *Marcus Eavis*

Previous page: **Straight out of school and onto the airfield! One of the author's first jobs was to organise minor works services at Heathrow, which presented the opportunity of taking a camera on 'airside' visits such as this one in September 1967. A Dan-Air Douglas DC-7 is being towed along 'Northside', passing the original brick control tower and the new Custom House.** *Author*

First published 2006

ISBN (10) 0 7110 3107 X
ISBN (13) 978 0 7110 3107 4

© Kevin McCormack 2006

Published by Ian Allan Publishing

an imprint of Ian Allan Publishing Ltd, Hersham, Surrey KT12 4RG
Printed in England by Ian Allan Printing Ltd, Hersham, Surrey KT12 4RG

Code: 0605/B1

Visit the Ian Allan Publishing website at www.ianallanpublishing.com

The City of London is a unique local authority: older than Parliament, it is non-party-political, has its own police force, runs three fee-paying schools, manages several open spaces outside London (*e.g.* Burnham Beeches) and maintains many historic traditions. The Corporation also grants the Freedom of the City of London to the great and the good (and others, such as your author, who, as a Freeman, is allowed to drive his sheep over London Bridge but has yet to do so, since he doesn't have any!).

For the purposes of this book (with the exception of one photograph) London is taken as extending to the boundaries of the London Boroughs, which means within a radius of some 15-18 miles from Charing Cross. Coverage begins in the West End, around The Strand and Trafalgar Square, and continues, with a certain amount of latitude, around the points of the compass: westwards towards Heathrow Airport, then south, east and north, before ending in the City and its environs.

The timespan of this book covers a 30-year period from 1949 to 1979, although the majority of images date from the 'Fifties and 'Sixties. There are some very rare colour views featuring events which are normally seen only in black and white — for example the Festival of Britain in 1951 and the Coronation decorations in 1953 — as well as street scenes depicting bygone transport such as double-deck trams, trolleybuses and horse-drawn carts. It has been a particular pleasure to include photographs of Heathrow in the pre-jet era, when passengers travelled in piston-engined airliners such as Constellations, Stratocruisers and Dakotas. In those days, as a young lad I used to ride there from Ealing on my pavement cycle, stopping off at the Hayes Novelty Shop in Coldharbour Lane to buy some stink bombs, and then 'plane spot' from the roof gardens and 'airside' coach tour. On leaving school, my first job was working for the Ministry of Aviation in the Central Area at Heathrow, and, again, memories come flooding back when I see these pictures and think of the people with whom I worked, the lunches (often liquid!) with Margaret, Thelma and Janet (not all at once!) and the chats about steam engines and buses with Vernon Murphy, a splendid photographer who is now a regular contributor to my books.

All the photographs are believed to be previously unpublished and, apart from a small selection of my own work (some taken while I was still at school), comprise material from the following photographers: Ian Stewart, Chris Evans, Neil Davenport, Marcus Eavis, Nick Lera, John Cramp, C. Carter, Bill Robertson, Roy Denison, Dave Edwards, Ken Allen, Mike Harries, Bruce Jenkins, Dave Brown, Vernon Murphy, J. Copland, E. J. McWatt and Miss Joyce Sharp. Grateful thanks are due to all these contributors and also to Martin Jenkins (Online Transport Archive), Ron White (Colour-Rail), Bob Bridger and Ian Pringle, for their valuable assistance.

Now sit back and enjoy nostalgic scenes of London and its transport, long before the advent of the Congestion Charge, counter-terrorist measures, articulated buses and other aspects of modern life.

Kevin R. McCormack
Ashtead, Surrey
April 2006

Left: **Raise a glass (or, in view of the backdrop, a pepper pot, perhaps) to the first prototype of a worldwide icon, the Routemaster bus. Unveiled to the public in September 1954 and placed in service in February 1956, RM1 pulls away from Charing Cross station in the Strand in 1958. The 'pepper-pots' belong to Coutts' Bank and form part of a triangular block designed by John Nash in 1830-2.** *Ian Stewart*

Below: **The Trafalgar Square fountains are gushing as another icon — an old-style Mini — pulls across RTL1363 in this unusual view looking south towards Whitehall. On the left is Nelson's column (erected in 1843), which together with the Square represents a memorial to Lord Nelson's victory in the Battle of Trafalgar in 1805.** *Ken Allen*

Above: Best known nowadays for the annual Trooping the Colour ceremony marking HM The Queen's official birthday, Horse Guards Parade has hosted various open-air exhibitions, such as this bus display to mark the Centenary of the London General Omnibus Co in 1956. With the trees of St James's Park in the background, this view dating from 21 July 1956 shows two double-decker buses with outside staircases — from left to right K424 built in 1920 and NS1995 dating from 1927. *Neil Davenport*

Right: Other buses on display at the Centenary included this horse-drawn vehicle and, to the right, B43 (nicknamed 'Ole Bill'), which served as a lorry on the Western Front during World War 1. The bus with the ventilation grilles in the roof and beneath the driver's canopy is RT2776, which toured North America in 1952. Behind 'Ole Bill' are the buildings comprising Horse Guards, once a guard-house for the former royal palace of Whitehall. Monarchs from Henry VIII to William III held Court there, but in 1698 fire destroyed all but Inigo Jones' Banqueting House, which survives today. *Neil Davenport*

Above: Static aircraft displays were also held on Horse Guards Parade, as demonstrated by this Gloster Gladiator biplane in 1960. Behind and to the right is Old Admiralty Building, where the author worked in the late 1970s/early 1980s and was able to enjoy grandstand views of Trooping the Colour. In the centre background the 'Grand Old' Duke of York, without his 10,000 men, stands 124ft high, as he has done since 1833. *Marcus Eavis*

Right: No tourists or street entertainers here — this is Covent Garden on 27 May 1970, when it was still a flower and vegetable market, before the main buildings, dating from 1830, were transformed into a shopping arcade. For some, the most interesting building today is the one with arched windows at the end of the street, because it houses London's Transport Museum! Most of the vehicles seen at the LGOC Centenary Parade reside there, along with many others. *Neil Davenport*

Left: Unexpectedly high car ownership after World War 2 meant that London Transport had ordered too many new buses and many were put in store, pending the withdrawal of older vehicles. After gathering dust for four years (and before application of its first advertisements) RTL1578 crosses Waterloo Bridge in August 1958. In the background, in the Strand, is Somerset House, built in 1775 as a home for various learned societies, later becoming government offices and now partly open to the public. *Ian Stewart*

Below left: A famous British steam locomotive (probably second only to *Mallard*, which holds the world speed record for steam), is *Flying Scotsman*, built in 1923. Here it is on 1 May 1968 leaving King's Cross station (alongside the contemporary 'Flying Scotsman' express) on a special commemorative non-stop run of 393 miles to Edinburgh. The mock-Gothic splendour in the background is St Pancras station, soon to be the new Eurostar terminus. *Author*

Right: There is plenty of activity at Waterloo station, gateway to the South West, in July 1964, as steam takes centre stage, without an electric train in sight. The locomotives are, from left to right, Nos 73082 *Camelot*, 34095 *Brentor*, 80095 and 34029 *Lundy*. Three years later Waterloo would bid farewell to British Railways steam services into London. *Author*

Left: Only a few trolleybus routes penetrated Central London, and none entered the West End, where unsightly poles and wires were considered unacceptable. Trolleybuses did, however, touch the City, and route 517 reached as far as Holborn. 'L3' No 1421 was photographed outside No17, Caledonian Road, King's Cross, in 1955. T. G. Lynes & Sons Ltd was founded in 1885 and traded from several premises in Caledonian Road. The company relocated to Enfield in 2003. *J. Copland / Online Transport Archive*

Right: To mark the Coronation of HM The Queen at Westminster Abbey on 2 June 1953 many roads in London were lavishly decorated. In this view of Fleet Street — an eastward continuation of the Strand which for many decades housed the newspaper industry — the dome of St Paul's Cathedral rises up through the bunting. Construction of this magnificent edifice began in 1675 and finished in 1710. Luckily, its architect, Sir Christopher Wren, lived to see its completion, reaching the age of 91 — a great achievement in those days (and even today). *Neil Davenport*

Left: With union flags proudly flying, a battered Wolseley car makes its way along The Mall towards Buckingham Palace as crowds gather in preparation for the Coronation. The backdrop is provided by Admiralty Arch, erected in 1910 at the Trafalgar Square end of The Mall as part of the national memorial to Queen Victoria. Admiral Lord Nelson looks down from the top left-hand corner of the picture. *Neil Davenport*

Right: Coronation crowds gather at Trafalgar Square; in the foreground, duly protected for the occasion, is the equestrian statue of King Charles I, which, to this day, has not moved from its plinth at the top of Whitehall since being placed there in 1676. It is from this point that mileages to/from London are measured. The statue stands on the site of the gothic cross in the village of Cheeringe which marked one of the points on the route of the funeral cortege of Queen Eleanor in 1290. A replica cross dating from 1865 stands in the forecourt of the aptly named 'Charing Cross' railway station. *Neil Davenport*

Above: This October 1969 view shows St Martin-in-the-Fields, completed in 1726 and replacing an earlier church on this once-rural site. The location of a church and churchyard here is said to have been at the behest of King Henry VIII, who took a dislike to funeral processions (memories of previous wives?) passing his Whitehall Palace windows to reach the burial ground at Westminster. The equestrian statue is of King George IV and was placed there temporarily in 1843 while a permanent site was found (they've given up looking!). The bus, RM2186, is operating on route 13, which was to retain its Routemasters until October 2005. *Mike Harries*

Right: For several years, starting in 1972, when this photograph was taken, a vintage bus service operated in Central London, normally using this 1930-built AEC Regent, ST922, which had been rescued from a scrapyard in 1966. This magnificent vehicle now lives at Cobham Bus Museum in leafy Surrey and no longer has to fight its way through the traffic congestion typified here at the junction of Whitehall and Trafalgar Square. *Marcus Eavis*

Below: RT3949 heads for the gap between the Austin taxi and the Rolls-Royce Silver Cloud as it crosses Piccadilly Circus on 26 May 1977. On the right is Shaftesbury Avenue, named after the Victorian philanthropist, the Earl of Shaftesbury, in whose memory the famous statue of Eros in the centre of the Circus was erected. *Chris Evans*

Right: Westminster Pier in 1961 also featuring Norman Shaw's New Scotland Yard standing on the Victoria Embankment. Originally built in 1890 and enlarged in 1907 in the same style, this striking building, now used as government offices, was the Headquarters of the Metropolitan Police until they moved to their present office block near Victoria in 1967. The *Clifton Castle*, built in 1926, still operates on the River Thames though much modified. *Author*

Left: Trams crossed Westminster Bridge until the system closed on 5 July 1952. This photograph taken in October 1949 depicts 'Feltham' No 2153 in the company of two older cars and clearly shows the slot between the rails through which the trams obtained electric power (the 'conduit system') in those parts of London where there were no overhead electric wires. *Bill Robertson / Colour-Rail LT125*

Right: An 'E1' tram turns onto Westminster Bridge from the Victoria Embankment in October 1949. The two leaping horses are pulling Boadicea's chariot — something they have been doing since 1902 (and without reins!). Westminster Bridge was built in 1862, while the Victoria Embankment, designed to cover a huge new sewer which diverted waste from entering the River Thames, was opened in 1870. In an attempt to create a 'Paris Match' the traffic-filled road may one day make way, at least at certain times of the year, for a pedestrian boulevard, with sand imported to create an artificial beach. *Bill Robertson / Colour-Rail LT117*

Left: Westminster Bridge has lost its trams here but there is still plenty to see in this view. The lorry is London Transport pole-carrier No 1080Q dating from 1958, the bus nearest the camera is an RTW, six inches wider than the other two buses, while the moped/motor-scooter riders will soon be compelled to wear crash helmets. Dominating the background are the Houses of Parliament, completed in 1857, their predecessors been having burned down in 1834 — an 'achievement' denied Guy Fawkes! The famous Clock Tower houses the bell, 'Big Ben', named after Sir Benjamin Hall, First Commissioner of Works when the bell was cast, and reputedly a large gentleman! *Ken Allen*

Right: The top end of Regent Street as lit up for Christmas 1963. Notice — perhaps with some difficulty, since he is not wearing a high-visibility jacket — the policeman on point duty directing the traffic, who is relying on the ends of his arms being seen! *Author*

Above: During the mid-1970s RT-type buses dating from 1947-54, which had been replaced by Routemasters on Central London services, suddenly reappeared on their old routes to cover shortages but, as RT3799 demonstrates here on 14 April 1977, these substitute RTs often carried ill-fitting or mangled blinds. The bus is negotiating Marble Arch, at the top end of Park Lane (visible in the background). Once the entrance to Buckingham Palace, the Arch was moved to its present site in 1851 to form a gateway to Hyde Park but nowadays finds itself marooned on a traffic island. *Chris Evans*

Right: Great excitement at Victoria station on 15 September 1963 — at the head of a special train visiting the Bluebell Railway in Sussex, and now residing in the Glasgow Transport Museum, is the famous Caledonian Railway Single (*i.e.* with a single pair of driving wheels). Built in 1886 for the Edinburgh Exhibition, this graceful machine was used in the Anglo-Scottish railway races of 1888 and withdrawn for preservation in 1935. Notice the whitewashed coal! *Bruce Jenkins*

Left: London's first 8ft-wide buses were the RTWs, of which 500 were built between 1949 and 1950. Intended for the busy inner-London routes, on which their wider gangways would be particularly useful, they were initially banned for being too big and relegated to the suburbs, being allowed into Central London only from 1951. Today big is best, and ironically the Routemaster, also 8ft wide, is considered small and narrow by current standards. RTW13 is seen in Victoria Street in August 1958. *Ian Stewart*

Below: A motley collection of coaches at Victoria coach station in 1958, the two nearest the camera belonging to the operator known as Midland Red. Next to them is a London Transport sightseeing coach, RFW15, waiting to operate a tour to London Airport (Heathrow). *Ian Stewart*

The replacement of rattling trams by smooth trolleybuses was a natural progression which enabled some of the electric infrastructure to be reused. In August 1959, with a Green Line RF coach in pursuit, 'F1' trolleybus No 741 rounds Shepherds Bush Green before returning to Uxbridge on what was then the nearest trolleybus route to the author's childhood home in Ealing.
Ian Stewart

'K1' trolleybus No 1126 leads an RTL and a Routemaster
along the southern side of Shepherds Bush Green
shortly before abandonment of London's trolleybus system
on 8 May 1962. *Nick Lera*

Left: The standard postwar London single-decker was the underfloor-engined RF type, introduced in 1951 and numbering 700 vehicles. Aside from those which were designated Green Line or Private Hire coaches, RFs were not seen in Central London, Hammersmith 'overground' station (built 1864), where RF488 was photographed on 10 June 1975

on route 290 from Richmond, being as close as they got to Central London. *Chris Evans*

Above: Watched by London Transport staff, 'K1' trolleybus No 1270 hurries along Chiswick High Road on a route 657 working from Hounslow to Shepherds Bush in spring 1962. *Nick Lera*

Above: In April 1962, before the Chiswick flyover became part of the M4 motorway, 'L3' trolleybus No 1524 makes its way to Hammersmith Broadway, accompanied by an AEC Mercury tower wagon (for working on the trolleybus overhead wires). Motor cars are represented by a Renault Dauphine and a Humber. *Nick Lera*

Right: Contrasting architectural styles dominate this view at Kew Bridge of trolleybus No 1524 heading back from Shepherds Bush on the last day of trolleybus operation in London. *Nick Lera*

Left: We head way out west for this photograph taken on 28 August 1967 of a Country Area bus displaying what would now be regarded as a controversial advertisement. RT3816 stands outside the Royal Mews at Windsor Castle, having worked a 457 service from Uxbridge. *Roy Denison*

Above: Welcome to the world's busiest international airport! London (Heathrow) Airport, as it was then known, looks decidedly deserted in this view dating from April 1963, with nothing visible on the stands save an 8-11-seater de Havilland Dove, forerunner of today's executive jet. *Author*

Below: Prospective airline passengers usually arrived by coach, but the normal method for spectators to reach Heathrow by public transport in the 1950s and '60s was to travel by Underground to Hounslow West (then the nearest Underground station) and catch the 81B bus. RT1134 is seen in August 1959 passing the Queen's Building, which gave access to the Exhibition Hall and the Roof Gardens. *Ian Stewart*

Right: Spectators view an approaching SABENA Douglas DC-3 Dakota from the Roof Gardens on 3 August 1957. This splendid attraction, which was built on the roofs of the Queen's Building and No 1 Passenger Building (now Terminal 2), was very popular with planespotters (and with shift workers for nocturnal trysts, so the story goes!). *Marcus Eavis*

Above: Flagship of the transatlantic fleets of BOAC and Pan Am during the 1950s was the Boeing Stratocruiser, a development of the military Superfortress. This ex-BOAC example, seen at Heathrow on 12 April 1958, is being operated temporarily by West African Airways Corporation; a BOAC Stratocruiser, with dark-blue tailplane, can be seen in the distance at the Northside terminal, together with a de Havilland Comet jet airliner and a Lockheed Constellation. *Marcus Eavis*

Right: Heathrow remained a tiny hamlet on the edge of Hounslow Heath even after the Fairey Aviation Co built the Great West Aerodrome in 1930. However, although the whole area was obliterated in 1944 by the present airport, Fairey's aircraft hangar, at the northern corner of the original site, survived for many years as a fire substation. In this 1959 view of a Portuguese Super Constellation and a BEA Viscount, the old hangar, reputed to have once been the largest in the world, is behind the BOAC advertising hoarding. *Marcus Eavis*

Above: Photographed in July 1967, this Douglas DC-3 Dakota freighter belonging to the Belgian national airline SABENA was operating one of the last regular services by this famous aircraft type into Heathrow. *Author*

Right: A little to the northeast of Heathrow was Heston Airport, where Britain's Prime Minister of the time, Neville Chamberlain, returning from Germany on 30 September 1938, held up his infamous piece of paper, declaring 'Peace in our time'. The airport, which opened in 1929, closed in 1946 due to its proximity to Heathrow. The M4 motorway and the adjacent Heston Services subsequently invaded much of the airport site, but the control tower and adjoining buildings survived until 1978. This view from 1970 features the author's Austin Seven cars, 'Aggie' and 'Charlotte', still much cherished today. *Author*

Left: The entrance to Heston Airport was located in the village of that name, where this photograph of some of the older parts (not a reference to Pamela, the pedestrian!) was taken in the summer of 1966. Electric bread-delivery vans such as that seen here were once a common sight. *Author*

Above: A peaceful suburban summer afternoon in 1962 — tennis players dressed correctly in white, retired gentleman tending his allotment, schoolgirl reading her comic beside a gas lamp and a Baker Street–Uxbridge Underground train about to enter Rayners Lane station. The train is composed of streamlined stock designed before World War 2, its flared bodywork intended to prevent passengers from hanging onto the outside. *Marcus Eavis*

Below: Not necessarily 'Ernie (the fastest milkman in the West)' of Benny Hill fame but certainly one of the last horse-drawn milk rounds in the London area. This early-morning shot of a Dalton's Farm Dairies delivery, taken in West Drayton Road, Hayes End, dates from December 1965. *Author*

Right: The routes around Kingston-upon-Thames were the first to have trolleybuses (in 1931) and the last (in 1962), and their base at the original tram depot at Fulwell now serves as a bus garage. This evocative evening shot depicts 'L3' No 1441 in Kingston town centre. *Martin Jenkins / Online Transport Archive*

Above: London's tram system would have ceased operation long before 1952 had it not been for the outbreak of World War 2, and replacement would have been by trolleybuses, as it had been up to 1939. However, the greater flexibility of motor buses evident during hostilities meant that they subsequently became the preferred alternative to trams and later went on to replace the trolleybuses as well. 'L3' trolleybus No 1405 glides over exposed tram lines in Station Road, Twickenham in May 1962. *Nick Lera*

Right: Hampton Court Palace, close to Kingston, was built for Cardinal Wolsey and was subsequently 'acquired' by Henry VIII. This view from 1959 captures the congestion which this major tourist attraction typically creates on summer Sundays and Bank Holidays. This impromptu advertisement for Ford cars also features 'L3' trolleybus No 1428 and two RT-type buses. *Ian Stewart*

Left: Chaos reigns in Kingston as a postwar 'Q1' trolleybus (which would later see service in Spain) suffers a de-wirement. Rectification is being attempted with the bamboo pole which was normally carried beneath the trolleybus in a tube resembling a narrow exhaust pipe. *Ian Stewart*

Below: Kingston was one of those towns on the edge of London where red and green buses came together. In this view at Wood Street bus station RT3140, operating on what would later become the author's local route through Ashtead, vies with RT3113 as to what film photographers should use while RF531 stands by. *Ian Stewart*

Left: A room with a view — Central Road, Worcester Park, in August 1972, as seen from the photographer's flat. Making its way to Sutton garage, RT1629 shows to advantage the sleek lines of the RT body, designed in the late 1930s. *Marcus Eavis*

Above: RT2619 climbs St John's Hill, Clapham Junction, on 29 May 1974. The imposing building behind the bus, boarded up in this view but subsequently restored, was once the station building and is inscribed with the name of the London, Brighton & South Coast Railway. *Chris Evans*

Above: Among the last horse-drawn vehicles to be seen regularly in London were the drays belonging to Young's and Whitbread, which served public houses in the vicinity of their respective London breweries. This mid-1960s photograph depicts a dray crossing the railway near Clapham Junction on its way from Young's 175-year-old Ram Brewery at Wandsworth, on which site beer has been brewed since 1581. *Vernon Murphy*

Right: A Whitbread horse-drawn dray making a delivery of beer in the summer of 1972. This location — Emerson Street, Southwark — is likely to be somewhat busier today, as visitors head for the nearby attractions of the Tate Modern or the replica of Shakespeare's Globe Theatre. Whitbread, founded in 1742, abandoned brewing in 2001. *Marcus Eavis*

Left: Between Sutton and Croydon lies Wallington, another location where red and green buses ran side by side, in the days before bus deregulation. RT3128 heads down Manor Road in the summer of 1973 on its journey from West Croydon to Chelsham bus garage, near Warlingham, in Surrey. *Dave Edwards*

Right: The RF type was London Transport's standard single-decker bus and coach of the 1950s and 1960s, the first examples entering service in 1951 and the last being withdrawn in 1979. This picture of RF392 was also taken in Manor Road, Wallington, the church seen on the previous page being visible in the background. *Dave Edwards*

Left: London's first major international airport was Croydon Airport, which replaced Hounslow Aerodrome after only a few months as the Customs Air Port of London in 1920. Created out of two adjacent airfields — Waddon and Beddington — and closed in September 1959, Croydon Airport was latterly unsuitable for any aircraft larger than the 14-17-seater de Havilland Heron, a four-engined stretched version of the Dove (see page 33). This view recorded on 8 August 1958 shows a Jersey Airlines Heron, G-AORG *Duchess of Brittany*, coming into land over Purley Way (the A23). *Marcus Eavis*

Below left: Also coming into land over Purley Way on the same day is Jersey Airlines Heron G-ANLN *Duchess of Guernsey*. Croydon had several large aircraft hangars, and it was a great thrill for the author when, together with his long-suffering mother and a schoolfriend, he was escorted around them in 1958 — spotting-book in hand, of course. *Marcus Eavis*

Right: This photograph, also taken at Croydon Airport on 8 August 1958, shows the Control Tower and public enclosure, including a girl dismantling a metal chair! Amazingly, since closure the airport has been anything but forgotten, despite much of its becoming a housing estate. The passenger buildings, control tower and Aerodrome Hotel still survive, and a Heron aircraft is mounted outside. Local buses even continue to terminate at 'Croydon Airport'. *Marcus Eavis*

Above: In September 1975 London's familiar red buses on route 190 gave way to the blue and cream of Southend Transport, whence 10 Leyland PD3 buses were borrowed to cover acute vehicle shortages, staying until February 1976. This view was recorded in High Street, Croydon, on 7 October 1975. *Chris Evans*

Right: When London Country took over London Transport's Country Area bus and Green Line coach services on 1 January 1970 there was at first no great visible change to the appearance of the existing fleet — nor, in many cases, for some considerable time. Until National Bus Company leaf green came along a slightly lighter version of LT Lincoln green was used, as evidenced by RML2316, working a 411 journey past Old Coulsdon pond on its way to West Croydon on 4 May 1978. *Chris Evans*

Left: Croydon still attracts transport enthusiasts today, but this is because it has the only tram system in London (new in 2000). Trams have now become very popular, whereas buses have lost favour. However, tram systems are expensive to install, so the latest money-saving idea is to design buses which look like trams! This Croydon scene from August 1959 depicts 'K1' trolleybus No 1069, dating from 1939, working the long (14-mile) route to Harlesden, in northwest London. *Ian Stewart*

Below: Moving across to the southeast of London, this is the free ferry carrying its load of road vehicles across the River Thames between Woolwich and North Woolwich in May 1963. This was in the days of the London Docks, as evidenced by the myriad cranes in the background. *Squires* was a paddle boat built in 1922 and is seen here in its final year of operation before replacement of the old steamers by modern diesel vessels. *Marcus Eavis*

Left: Woolwich presented the extraordinary sight of London double-deck buses threading their way through the market stalls in Beresford Square (and over the cobbles and disused tram lines). Regardless of the inevitable fumes, shoppers survey the goods on offer as RT3817 and, following at a distance, RT1755 make their way to Bexleyheath. *Chris Evans*

Below: Another reminder of London's days as a thriving port. The view east from London Bridge, looking down the River Thames, would now include the warship, HMS *Belfast*, in the middle of the river, and the Mayor of London's City Hall on the right, with not a dockyard crane in sight. Tower Bridge, opened in 1894, still dominates the scene today. *Ken Allen*

Left: Wanstead Flats, near Leytonstone, is not a high-rise development but a large open space in northeast London. This period photograph from 1949 shows the funfair — a regular attraction, with rides costing as little as 3d (1¼p). *C. Carter*

Right: A reminder of the standard London double-decker bus which the RT class replaced. STL1761 entered service in January 1937 and is seen here in 1949 in Eastern Avenue, Gants Hill, on its way to Leytonstone. *C. Carter*

Below: Still fitted with an original-style Weymann roofbox body, RT458, which entered service in December 1947, shares route 9 with brand-new Routemaster RM95 at Becontree Heath in August 1959. Route 9 is still operated by Routemasters between Aldwych and the Royal Albert Hall. *Ian Stewart*

Left: London still had docks in 1961, when this picture was taken, because the trolleybus says so! 'K1' No 1105, dating from 1939, stands at the terminus of route 647 at Stamford Hill, south of Tottenham. A bamboo pole, used in the event of planned or accidental de-wirings, is attached to the trolleybus stop.
Marcus Eavis

Above: Edgware was the last haven for the postwar but archaic-looking TD-class Leyland Tigers, which ran until 8 October 1962. TD95, now lovingly restored by Cobham Bus Museum in Surrey, has just passed a classmate in Hale Lane on the last day of TD operation. *John Cramp*

Another shot taken on the last day of TD operation by London Transport, 8 October 1962. The vehicle is a resplendent-looking TD105, the location once again Hale Lane. The TD class was introduced only five years earlier than the RF class but looked 25 years older! *John Cramp*

Trolleybus operation to Edgware was just about to end when the
photographer snapped 'N1' No 1642 at the terminus of route 666
to Hammersmith on 29 December 1961. Services ceased
on 2 January 1962 in a blizzard. *John Cramp*

Left: Funeral rites are performed at Wood Green on the final day of trolleybus operation there — 8 November 1961 — as enthusiasts with flares guide the last vehicle, 'K2' No 1353, into the depot. *E. J. McWatt / Online Transport Archive*

Above: Early 1970s homo sapiens, displaying the latest in sartorial elegance, strides away as RT3884 pulls into Golders Green station forecourt. Dark-green poles with knobs on are evidence of a lost civilisation — trolleybuses. *Dave Brown*

Left: There were just a few days left of trolleybus operation at North Finchley when this shot was taken in late October 1961, the final date of operation being 7 November. RM733 serves as a portent of things to come. *Ian Stewart*

Below: Ex-Metropolitan Railway electric locomotive No 4 *Lord Byron* prepares to back onto an Aylesbury-bound Metropolitan Line Underground train at Baker Street station in 1959. This powerful locomotive was one of a batch of 20 built in 1922/3, most of the class surviving in passenger service until 1961. Two — No 5 *John Hampden* and No 13 *Sarah Siddons* — have been preserved, but not No 8 *Sherlock Holmes*, named after Baker Street's famous fictional resident. *Marcus Eavis*

Below: Pictured in October 1949, 'E3' tram No 101 (ex-Leyton Corporation No 181) nears Holborn, heading towards the Kingsway Subway incline leading to the Victoria Embankment via an opening in the side of Waterloo Bridge. The incline, tram tracks and iron railings are still *in situ* today in the middle of Southampton Row, but the remainder of the subway has been abandoned or converted into an underpass. *Bill Robertson / Colour-Rail LT110*

Right: In 1951, 100 years on from the Great Exhibition in Hyde Park, the Festival of Britain was held on the South Bank of the River Thames. The Festival occupied a 27-acre site on either side of Hungerford Railway Bridge (seen in the middle distance in this view), which links Waterloo East and Charing Cross stations. The author was taken to the Festival as a small boy (and still has a souvenir ticket to prove it) but cannot remember anything about it! Much of the site is now covered by high-rise blocks, although Londoners can still enjoy the legacy of the Royal Festival Hall, the top of which is just visible on the far right. *C. Carter*

Left: The building behind the recumbent Henry Moore sculpture lived on for a time after the Festival as an airline terminal for British European Airways (BEA), as seen in the next picture, until superseded by one in West London (Gloucester Road). *C. Carter*

Below: Three of BEA's distinctive one-and-a-half-deck airport coaches, with rear passenger section raised above the luggage compartment, congregate outside the Waterloo air terminal ready to take passengers to Heathrow in 1957. The building in the background (on the extreme left) is the former hospital seen overleaf. *Marcus Eavis*

Left: Moving south of the river to Waterloo, we encounter RTL299 having just come off Waterloo Bridge in January 1968, the final year of RTL operation. Somerset House, across the river, can just be glimpsed in the distance on the extreme left, while the brick building behind the bus, still extant today, is the former Royal Waterloo Hospital for Children and Women. Although the Leyland RTLs carried bodies identical to those on the AEC RTs they were fewer in number, and their running units (engines etc) effectively became non-standard as the RT family diminished. *Roy Denison*

Right: This view from Blackfriars Bridge, recorded on 11 August 1976, features Alexandra Bridge, the iron lattice-work structure opened in 1864 which has now been replaced by an adjacent modern railway bridge. Sir Christopher Wren's masterpiece, St Paul's Cathedral, rises up behind RT563, seen heading for Merton garage after a rush-hour working to Victoria Embankment. *Chris Evans*

Left: Dating from the autumn of 1964, this tranquil view of Waterloo Bridge from the Victoria Embankment features the purpose-built Royal Research Ship *Discovery*. Launched in Dundee (where it is now displayed) on 21 March 1901, this vessel, commanded by Captain Scott, took part in the successful National Antarctic Expedition of 1901-4. It was not, however, involved in the tragic Polar Expedition of 1910-12, perhaps best remembered for Capt Oates' immortal words 'I am just going outside and may be some time'. *Author*

Above: The Victoria Embankment, looking towards the Houses of Parliament, as seen through Hungerford railway bridge from Platform 6 of Charing Cross station on 8 May 1962. The bus, which appears to be RT4213, is on its way to Abbey Wood on route 177. Having crossed the Thames by means of Westminster Bridge, it will shortly cross back via Blackfriars Bridge.
Joyce Sharp

Typifying the magnificent steam locomotives which hauled Anglo-Scottish expresses in and out of London from the mid-1930s to the early 1960s, aptly named No 46245 rests at Willesden depot in northwest London during April 1964. Three of these 'Coronation' Pacifics have survived the scrapman's torch: *Duchess of Hamilton*, *Duchess of Sutherland* and *City of Birmingham. Author*